D1291726

*First published in
the United States in 1990 by*
Gloucester Press
387 Park Avenue South
New York NY 10016

Design David West
         Children's Book Design
Editorial Planning Clark Robinson Ltd
Editor Bibby Whittaker
Researcher Cecilia Weston-Baker
Illustrated by Alex Pang

EDITORIAL PANEL

The author, Howard Timms, is an
expert on computers and their
applications.

The educational consultant, Peter
Thwaites, is principal of
Northaw School, Salisbury,
Wiltshire.

The editorial consultant, John
Clark, has contributed to many
information and reference books.

Library of Congress Cataloging-in-Publication Data

Timms, Howard.
   Living in the future.

   (Today's world)
   Summary: Speculates on living conditions of the
future and shows how current technology, such as
robotics, computers, and alternative energy
sources, can affect future health care, shopping,
leisure, and work.
   1. Technological innovations--Juvenile literature.
[1. Technological innovation. 2. Forecasting] I. Title.
II. Series: Today's world (New York, N.Y.)
T173.8.T56   1990   89-81610
ISBN 0-531-17224-4

TODAY'S WORLD

LIVING IN THE FUTURE

HOWARD TIMMS

GLOUCESTER PRESS
New York · London · Toronto · Sydney

CONTENTS

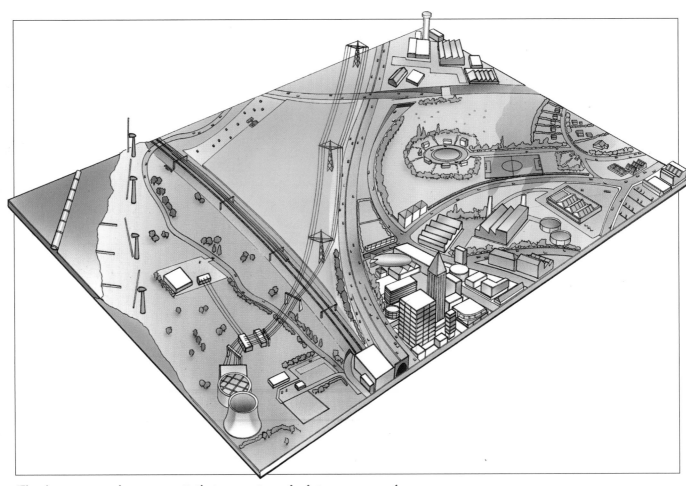

The front cover shows an artist's impression of a future space colony.

INTRODUCTION

With the exception of Australia, New Zealand and Japan, today's most highly developed countries are in the West. Collectively, all of these countries, including Japan, are known as the Western Nations. This book is about the way in which life and work in the Western nations can be expected to change within the reader's lifetime. It examines some of the latest developments, predicting the effect they will have on people's lifestyles in the next 20, 30 or 40 years. Similar changes will eventually take place in the developing countries, although they will take longer. Many machines now in homes are partly automatic, and in many countries this trend will continue so that before very long a whole home will be automatic. Computers are being applied ever more widely, and there will be further developments in homes, leisure, work and transportation. Technological changes may cause problems, such as pollution and shortage of resources, and these are unlikely to disappear. Some new answers should develop soon. One possibility is to move people away from Earth into space, and to obtain resources from the Moon and other heavenly bodies.

A futuristic house in the American desert uses wind and solar panels.

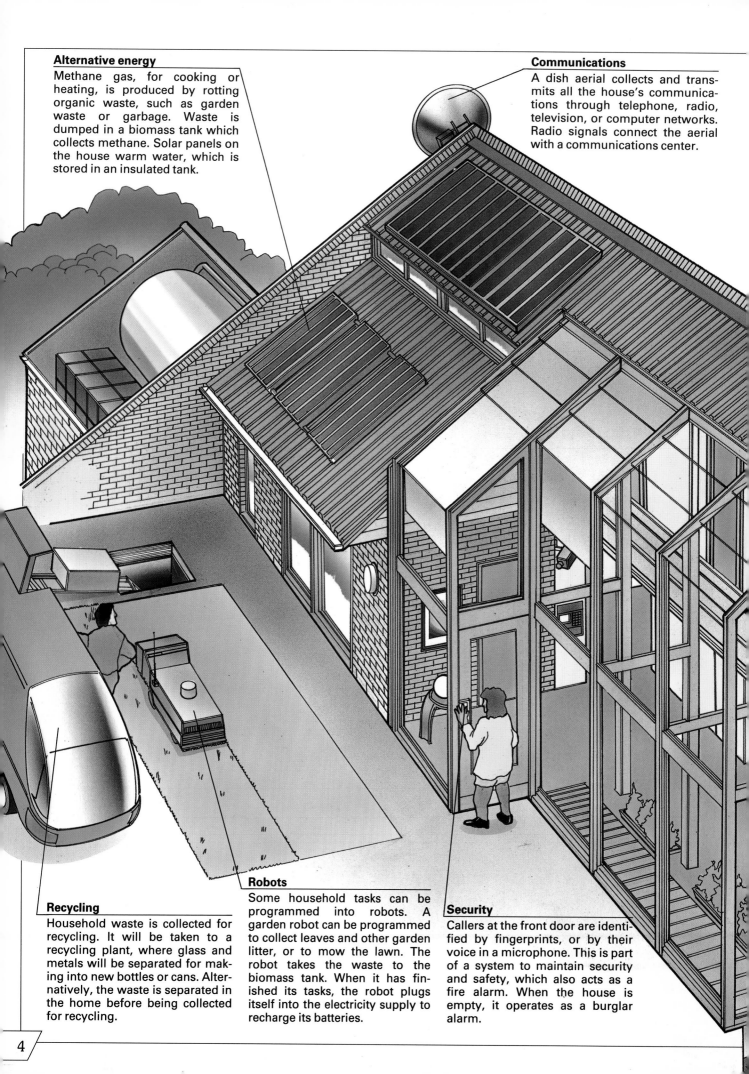

Alternative energy

Methane gas, for cooking or heating, is produced by rotting organic waste, such as garden waste or garbage. Waste is dumped in a biomass tank which collects methane. Solar panels on the house warm water, which is stored in an insulated tank.

Communications

A dish aerial collects and transmits all the house's communications through telephone, radio, television, or computer networks. Radio signals connect the aerial with a communications center.

Recycling

Household waste is collected for recycling. It will be taken to a recycling plant, where glass and metals will be separated for making into new bottles or cans. Alternatively, the waste is separated in the home before being collected for recycling.

Robots

Some household tasks can be programmed into robots. A garden robot can be programmed to collect leaves and other garden litter, or to mow the lawn. The robot takes the waste to the biomass tank. When it has finished its tasks, the robot plugs itself into the electricity supply to recharge its batteries.

Security

Callers at the front door are identified by fingerprints, or by their voice in a microphone. This is part of a system to maintain security and safety, which also acts as a fire alarm. When the house is empty, it operates as a burglar alarm.

THE FUTURE HOUSE

A hundred years ago, a few houses had servants who cleaned, and kept fires going for heat. Now many homes have machines which do cleaning, heating and other work. Increasingly, future homes will have robots and computer-controlled systems for running the home.

The house of the future will be easy to run. Already the time needed to look after the cleaning of a home, and to make it comfortable, is getting ever smaller. Machines such as automatic washing machines, dishwashers, and vacuum cleaners make household jobs quicker. In future, robots will be able to do more than one task, and will be able to move around. As already happens in some factories, robots will be controlled and programmed by a computer, making sure that the machines do exactly what the householder wants. Fuels such as oil and gas are getting scarce, and future homes will be built to produce some, or even all, of their own energy.

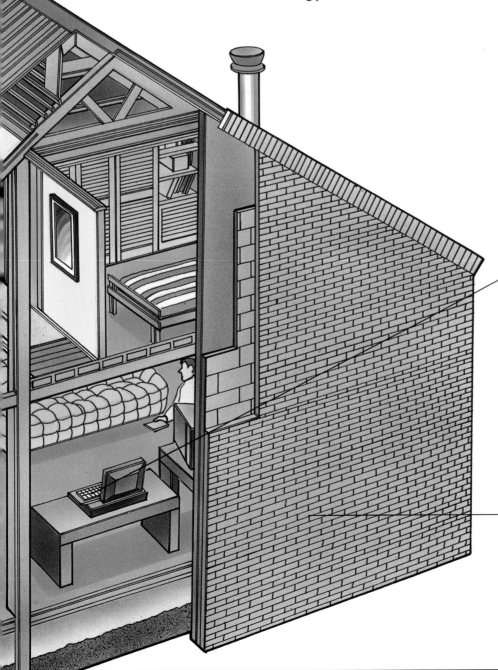

The house of tomorrow will run itself. A computer controls heating, safety, cleaning, conservation of energy and materials, production of energy, and communications. Robots controlled by the computer do household chores. The computer senses when the occupants are out, provides burglar and fire alarm systems, and keeps the place clean and tidy.

Computer control

A central computer controls the main systems, such as security, energy production, or internal heating and lighting. It controls the house temperature by altering things like the reflectiveness of window blinds, or air circulation, or by burning heating fuel when needed. The computer can switch lights on automatically when someone enters a room. It receives the householders' instructions for robots, and programs them.

Materials

Better building materials make the house cheaper and easier to run. An example is window glass, strong and long lasting, and with good insulation. Special glass can be made whose reflection properties are computer-controlled to stop glare from the Sun, or to absorb or reflect heat as needed.

5

COMPUTERS IN THE HOME

When electronic calculators first became available, they cost over one hundred and sixty dollars. But now they cost only a few dollars. Robots for the home will be very expensive to begin with. But perhaps one day as many homes will have a robot as have a washing machine today.

Day to day life in the home of the future will be different in many ways from that of today. Because tasks will be undertaken by computers and robots, people will have extra time for leisure and social activities. Computers will even help to plan each person's day. They will also start doing jobs that have not been done before, such as controlling the internal environment of the home – the heating, lighting and ventilation. Although life will be made easier in many ways, people will have to learn new skills so that they will be able to tell the machines exactly what they want them to do.

Central control

Occupants of future homes will not need to make decisions about turning on lights, or turning up heating or ventilation. A central computer will do it for them. It uses sensors, connected by wires, to find out if lighting levels are sufficient, or if the temperature is correct, and adjusts the lights or heating if necessary. Similarly, when the occupants are away, the computer's security sensors check whether there are any intruders. If there are, it contacts the police.

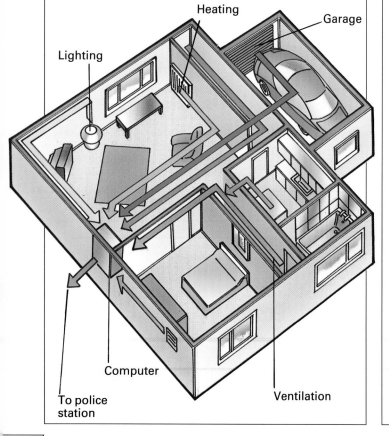

Lighting

Heating

Garage

Computer

To police station

Ventilation

Computer management

Managing a home includes keeping check on the costs of running it, a job that computers make easy. But the range of home management jobs that computers can help with is growing all the time. Shopping by computer is possible for a wide range of goods and services. A customer at home shops by linking the home computer by phone to a large central computer. Information on goods and prices is passed to the home computer for the customer to study. Orders for goods are then passed to the computer network, which notifies stores to supply the required goods directly to the customer's home. Money to pay for the goods is deducted directly from the customer's bank account.

Ordering goods using a home computer

Robots

Any machine that controls itself is a robot. Many houses now have machines which are robotic – an example is an automatic washing machine. Each robot stores a program (a set of instructions) which it carries out whenever it is switched on. Generally, home robots carry more than one program, and users of the robot can select the program they need. More intelligent robots choose instructions depending on circumstances. An automatic vacuum cleaner, for example, controls its own movement. The robot's sensors tell it if something is in its way, and the robot decides whether to reverse or go around it. After a time, the robot learns the layout of the house and plans the best route around.

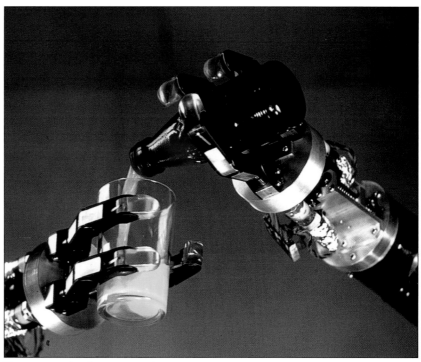

Pouring a drink is a simple task for a robot.

Less waste

A group of homes, such as a block of apartments, can already have an economical system for reusing most household waste. A system which has been used in Sweden since the 1960s has a pneumatic pipe to carry garbage along to a separator. Compressed air is used to push the garbage along the pipe. The separator sorts out metal and glass garbage into separate containers. The glass and metal are taken away to special factories where they can be recycled.

Any part of the garbage that will burn is piped along to a heating plant. Burning the waste produces heat which is used to make steam. More pipes carry the steam, which is used for heating the building.

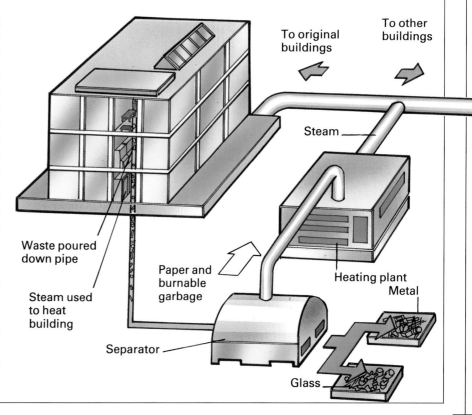

To original buildings

To other buildings

Steam

Waste poured down pipe

Paper and burnable garbage

Steam used to heat building

Heating plant

Metal

Separator

Glass

LIVING IN A COMMUNITY

Many of the world's largest cities provide homes for more than 10 million people. Within cities, individual communities consist of groups of only a few thousand people, similar in population to a small town. In remote country districts, a community may consist of only a very few families.

Homes are generally part of a community, such as a neighborhood within a city or one of its suburbs. Most communities include some services such as stores or libraries. Many people want their home to be near the services or places that they visit regularly. But some people either cannot afford a home near a town center, or prefer to live nearer the country. Others, such as farmers, have to live in the country. For these people, it is usually more convenient to be able to do a lot of varied shopping, or use several services, in one place on one trip.

Communities

The success of a community depends on the way that its planners arrange its parts in relation to each other. Planning for homes to be close together means that each will use less land and be cheaper. But the inhabitants may suffer noise and lack of privacy. Many high-rise apartments built during the 1950s and 1960s were not supplied with services, such as stores and leisure facilites. High rises consisting only of apartments are rarely built now. The few that are built include services or have them nearby. Town layouts for the future allow for space around each home, with schools and services nearby, good transportation connections, and amenities like libraries, shopping centers, leisure complexes and parks within walking distance.

Old high rises are being demolished.

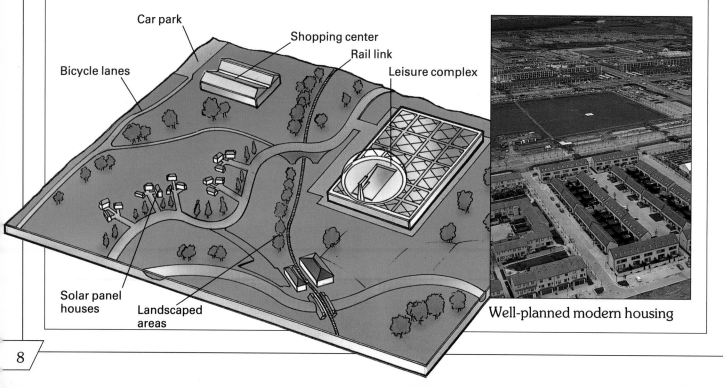

Car park

Shopping center

Rail link

Bicycle lanes

Leisure complex

Solar panel houses

Landscaped areas

Well-planned modern housing

Schools

In schools of the future, children will still have to be taught basic skills, such as reading, writing and counting. But many skills, such as dealing with money or crossing roads, will be taught partly by computer. By using programs which allow the individual to interact with the words or pictures, computers can help students to learn at their own pace. Some programs will use simulations to make situations seem like real life. Because computers will be such a major part of school life, they will affect the ways in which many subjects are taught. Teachers will have more time for individual tuition, and students will have more time to study a wide variety of subjects.

A student doing homework on a computer

A computer helping to teach languages

Stores

Shopping in bulk, or for a variety of goods, becomes increasingly easy with the development of shopping arcades and malls. A shopping mall includes many small stores, which sell a wide variety of goods, as well as larger stores. In future, a customer visiting a shopping center will be able to use a centralized delivery service. Goods from various stores will be taken to a central collection area, packed and delivered together. They will also be charged for together, with a computer system reading bar code numbers on each item. The computer will arrange for payment on the goods to each of the stores from which they were bought.

A large shopping center in Toronto, Canada

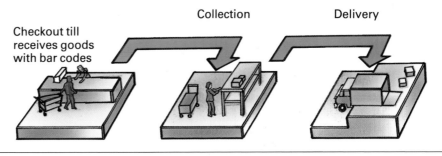
Checkout till receives goods with bar codes   Collection   Delivery

Healthcare has improved greatly over the last 50 years. Much of this is a result of advanced technology. Surgeons can now use lasers to perform operations that could not be carried out before. Computer technology is used to detect illnesses before they become serious.

Improvements in medicine have led to people being fitter and living longer lives. New techniques in biotechnology, such as genetic engineering, allow the production of "tailor-made" drugs and vaccines. The benefits will continue in the future through developments such as automation in surgery, which will use computer control and robotics to perform operations.

People's health is also improving because of better preventive medicine, which involves monitoring a patient's state of health, and encouraging healthy activities. More and more people regard preventive medicine as something they can take advantage of without a doctor – for example, by eating a balanced diet of healthy foods. A keep-fit plan is one area in which computer technology is likely to bring continuing improvements.

Keeping healthy

Keeping fit through exercise is best done to a plan, and figures need to be worked out for the correct amount of exercise at each stage. Progress in health terms can be measured through pulse and breathing rates, and blood pressure. A computer is ideal for taking and recording all these measurements and planning future exercise. Another approach to better health involves routine screening, in which a person is examined regularly to detect possible signs of a disorder before it becomes difficult to treat.

1.

2.
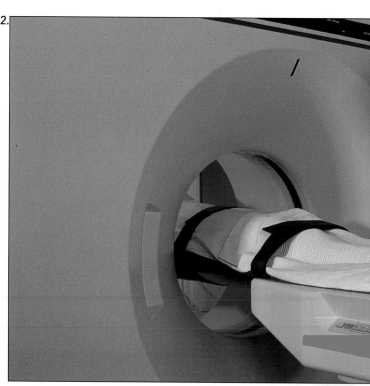

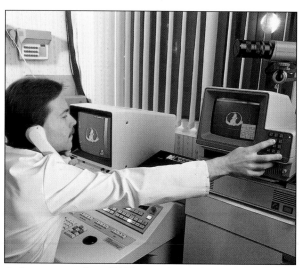

A doctor sends a CAT scan by videophone.

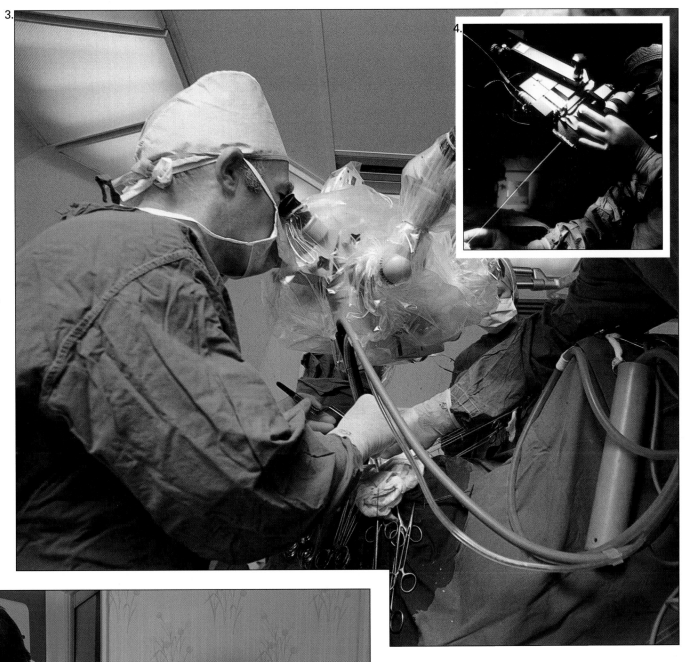

Future medicine will make increasing use of high technology for the investigation and diagnosis of illnesses, as well as for their treatment. 1. An operator uses a computer system to analyze data about a patient's bone structure. 2. This patient is having a CAT scan. CAT stands for computerized axial tomography, which is a technique for taking "pictures" of tissues inside the body. The scanner moves around the patient and takes very detailed X rays of cross-sections of the body. 3. In microsurgery, the surgeon uses a microscope to perform delicate operations on nerves and other small structures. 4. A laser beam is being employed to treat tumors inside a patient's ear.

Future developments in computer games will include new output devices. These enable the computer to make special images such as holograms (a three-dimensional image made using laser technology).

In your own home you can tour the Universe, fight a dragon, or fly an airplane, by playing computer games. Even better is a three-dimensional image, or a chair that gives you the feeling of a moving spacecraft. This kind of realism is now available in pilot training simulators, and will soon be available in homes for learning a whole range of skills, such as learning how to sail a wind-surfer.

For leisure out of the home, more people will visit theme parks. And with faster and cheaper air travel, tourism will expand as more people take vacations abroad.

Home entertainment

A link between a computer and a videodisk produces interactive video (IV). When used as part of a video game, interactive video could show actual moving images of real places as part of the game. Another use of IV could be choosing a holiday, with the opportunity to explore as you wish the places that you are considering visiting. After choosing a place, you might decide to use IV to learn the local language. You could practice asking people for directions. When you try following the directions in an IV simulation, you'll soon know if you understood them.

Other educational uses of video enable people to learn about the arts. Paintings can be studied, and holograms would display sculpture and architecture in realistic three dimensions. Using IV, it will be possible to learn how to play a musical instrument. Many games and sports can be simulated, for example to improve a player's skill at chess or pool before taking on a human opponent. Three-dimensional war games using holograms (right) will replace today's flat-screen versions.

This computer responds to a child's spoken instructions.

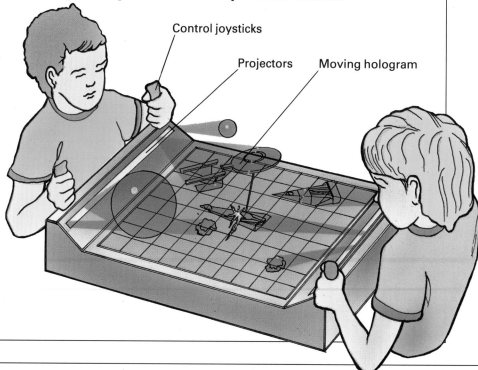

Control joysticks

Projectors   Moving hologram

Total sensory simulation

You are an airline pilot, making your first landing at Hong Kong. As the runway lights come nearer, you move the throttle controls to reduce engine power. You feel the aircraft respond, and engine noise decreases. You are in a real cockpit, and your senses tell you just what they would tell you in a real aircraft, but you are in a simulator. A computer responds to your actions in the cockpit, and provides total sensory simulation of flying. The images of Hong Kong are on a screen in front of you, hydraulic rams move the cockpit, and loudspeakers provide the sound. All the seats in a movie theater can be similarly controlled (right) to give a sensation of movement.

A pilot "flying" an aircraft simulator

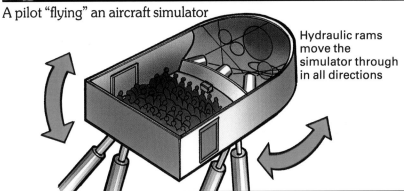

Hydraulic rams move the simulator through in all directions

Container vacation

Campers are a popular method of cheap, mobile vacationing. But campers sit idle and unused for much of the year, while their owners are at home, sometimes short of space. The solution is to link the camper onto the home, with a connecting door, and plug-in electrical and plumbing services. The house then has one more bathroom, and another living room or guest room. The camper would be moved on a transporter to its vacation site.

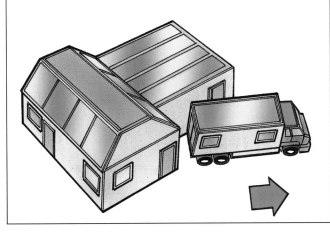

Theme vacation

Theme parks use technology similar to that in pilot training simulators, and give vacationers the thrill of realistic trips to exciting or dangerous places. As well as projected images, sound effects and simulated movement, theme parks may use realistic moving models and androids – robots that look like humans. Computer control ensures that effects are timed for maximum impact, or to provide interactive response with the vacationers.

Theme park Alton Towers, England

13

AT WORK

Factories with complete automation, where no people work, already exist and will probably soon be common. Raw materials and components are fed into one end of the production line, and finished goods come out at the other end. Offices, too, make increasing use of computers and electronic equipment. As a result, people can do office work from home, and send out the results of their work as "electronic mail" using data links.

A completely automated factory can make a variety of products, all literally untouched by human hands. Automatic hover platforms carry materials around the factory. Machines do the assembly, and can work 24 hours a day if necessary. Occasionally they may stop for repairs and maintenance, but even that work they may do themselves. Although no people work in manufacturing, human beings still do the most important work of all – managing the factory and deciding what to make. Managers monitor the factory's output and customers' needs, and plan the type and quantity of product to be made. Plans are fed to the main factory computer, and are processed into instructions for the machines in the factory. Managers also ensure that raw materials and components are available, normally ordering the quantities suggested by the computer system.

Robot technology

Robots are machines that continually carry out instructions stored in their memory. Like human beings, robots have ways of sensing what they are doing. They may use their sensors to take measurements, or to discover if a stage of production is complete. The information from sensors goes back to the robot in a process called feedback. The robot uses the feedback to decide what to do next to carry out its instructions. Robots are well suited to doing boring and repetitive work. Some can be programmed to do a variety of different tasks.

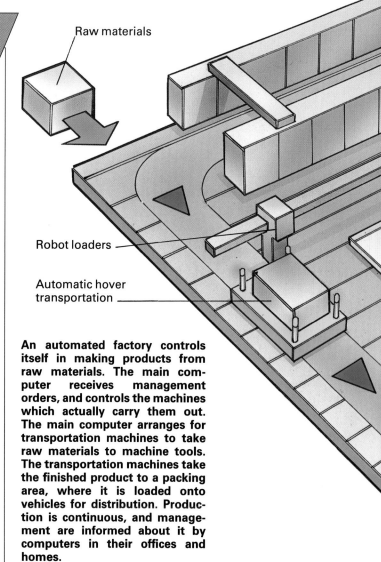

Raw materials

Robot loaders

Automatic hover transportation

An automated factory controls itself in making products from raw materials. The main computer receives management orders, and controls the machines which actually carry them out. The main computer arranges for transportation machines to take raw materials to machine tools. The transportation machines take the finished product to a packing area, where it is loaded onto vehicles for distribution. Production is continuous, and management are informed about it by computers in their offices and homes.

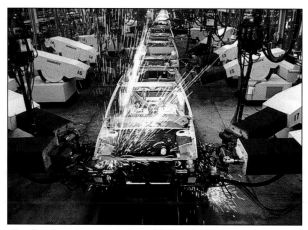

Car bodies being welded by robots

At home

A manager needs to keep in touch all the time with an automated factory because production can go on 24 hours a day. Using a computer at home, the manager can link with factory computers, and obtain information from them. If decisions are needed to change products or materials, the manager inputs information on the home computer, and it is passed on to the factory.

Input computer

At the office

Plans for factory output are regularly revised by the office computer as a result of customers' orders, changes in price or availability of raw materials. Revised plans – possibly developed by somebody working entirely at home – are fed into the office input computer which passes them to the main factory computer.

Tool store

Multitool computer

Input computer

Control computer

Automatic machine tool

Finished article

Main computer

Electronic guide rail

At the factory

Under the control of the main computer, the machine tools keep producing goods, stopping only to receive new instructions, or to be given different tools when a different type of product is to be made. A multitool computer works out the tools necessary for individual tasks, and selects them from the tool store. Hovercraft automatically carry everything that travels to or from the machine tools.

Growth of service industries

Using robots frees people for jobs that only human beings can do. Many such jobs involve providing a service for other people, and these workers are said to be in the service industries. They provide services such as cleaning, selling or retailing, hotels and catering, as well as banking, education, law and government, and many others. Most workers in these areas meet customers or clients, and provide a service for which they charge money. For example, a lawyer charges a fee for giving advice or representing you in court. Computers and other technology already make service industries more efficient, and in future robots will probably make them even more so.

Interior of a modern American hotel

Dangerous jobs

Some work is impossible for human beings to do, like assembling radioactive parts of a nuclear reactor. Such work can only be done by remote control, using robots which can operate without damage in a radioactive place. The work is supervised from behind protective screens or walls by technicians who watch progress by television and control the equipment. Another example of risky work done by robots is mining in very narrow seams, where robots can extract coal or other minerals in places too cramped or unstable for people to be safe. Bomb disposal robots approach a bomb without any risk to the robot operator. They can pick up a bomb and place it in a bomb-proof container, to be defused.

A bomb disposal robot picks up a suspect suitcase

Vital services

In an emergency such as a fire, accident, or crime in the home, people's safety depends on how quickly they can contact the emergency services. Fire, ambulance, and police services will leave their base to help as soon as they receive a message. A vital part of the message is the exact location of the emergency, and much time may be lost giving addresses, and working out the best route. One way of saving time is a radio transmitter attached to a fire or security alarm. In an emergency it will automatically transmit details of the location. A fire engine with a radio receiver will be able to take the location message and its on-board computer will show the location of the fire and the best route to it. Ambulance crews will radio the hospital to give details of a victim's injuries.

Control center at a police station

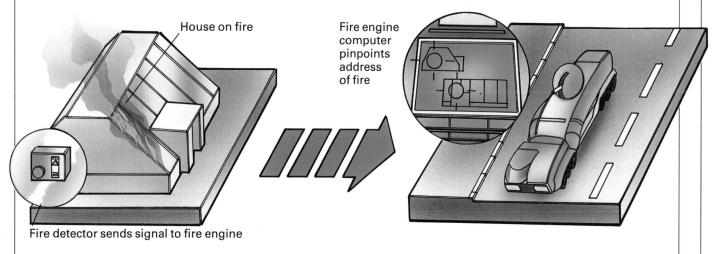

House on fire

Fire engine computer pinpoints address of fire

Fire detector sends signal to fire engine

Criminals

Electronic monitoring is a way of restricting criminals' freedom with less expense than putting them in prison. A belt, fitted around the criminal's ankle, carries an electronic device which sends out a coded radio signal. The receiver for the signal is a special telephone fitted in the criminal's home. If the criminal tries to leave home, the signal is broken, and the telephone automatically contacts the police. Electronic monitoring is particularly useful for people awaiting trial for crimes, and who may be found to be innocent. The police can ensure that they will come for trial with no risk of imprisoning innocent people.

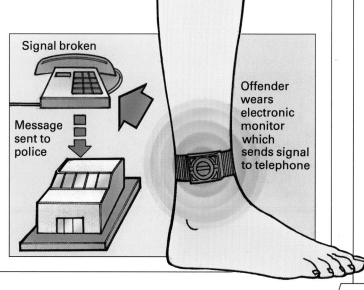

Signal broken

Message sent to police

Offender wears electronic monitor which sends signal to telephone

Farming and food

Farming was one of the first industries to be mechanized, with machines for threshing and harvesting. It was also one of the first to use solar power, in greenhouses. In recent years, many advances have come from the development of better livestock and types of plant through the use of genetic engineering. The results include food animals that mature more quickly, and crop plants that tolerate cold climates or poor rainfall. But it looks as if the next developments may be computerization and automation, already widespread in manufacturing industries. Future farms will use robots for harvesting, milking cows, or monitoring grain in store.

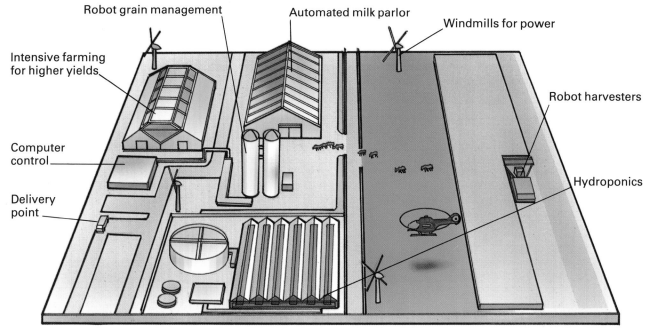

Robot grain management

Intensive farming for higher yields

Computer control

Delivery point

Automated milk parlor

Windmills for power

Robot harvesters

Hydroponics

Irradiated potatoes do not sprout in store.

Growing plants without soil using hydroponics

Applying new technology to farms may include a form of electronic monitoring, by which a computer will record not only a cow's location, but also its activity and health. Intensive crop farming will include hydroponics, growing plants without soil. The plants are supported in a wire mesh and are fed entirely by water containing a computer-controlled mixture of chemicals. Preserving farm produce may be done by irradiation, in which radioactivity kills bacteria, bugs and mold, and also slows down ripening and sprouting.

Cows wearing collars with electronic monitors

The city

A vertical city with homes, offices, factories, stores and recreational facilities all under one roof is perfectly possible with skyscraper technology. Many buildings and developments already have enough space to house a small town, especially in the United States. Homes, stores and offices are together, linked by corridors and lifts. The whole building can efficiently be kept warm in winter and cool in summer, so that travel to work within the building will be easy and pleasant. Alternatives, especially in countries such as Japan that are running out of living space on land, include floating cities built on artificial islands and underwater cities in watertight domes on the seabed. The island would be connected to the mainland by a causeway or a bridge carrying a road and a high-speed rail link. An underwater city would have elevator shafts up to the surface, with a landing platform for helicopters or vertical takeoff aircraft. Eventually it may be possible to construct a city in space or on the Moon.

A design for a mile-high skyscraper

Computer future

The rapid pace of developments in computers in the 1970s and 1980s is almost certain to continue right through the 1990s and into the 2000s. As the memory chips become more efficient, the average size of computers will continue to decrease. Wristwatch computers will soon combine timekeeping with a diary, address book and notepad. Higher priced watches will also give the user a link to other computers and to the telephone network. They will use voice communication. Human speech will tell the computer what to do, and the computer will report back to its operator through a speech synthesizer.

Improved memory, and new software, will soon give computers artificial intelligence, so that they can think, ask questions, and solve problems without having to be given detailed instructions. Computers will also be able to automatically translate from one language to another. This development will greatly improve communications throughout the world.

Another *very* futuristic idea involves connecting nerve cells directly to a computer's memory.

How a nerve cell might grow on a silicon chip.

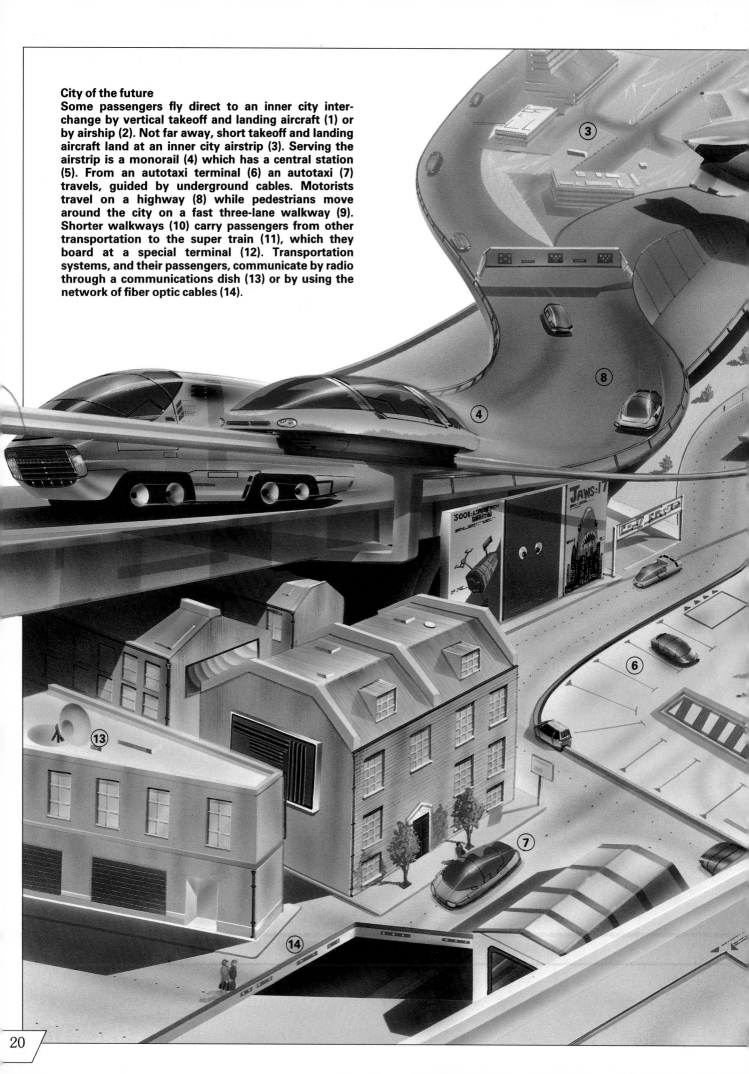

City of the future
Some passengers fly direct to an inner city interchange by vertical takeoff and landing aircraft (1) or by airship (2). Not far away, short takeoff and landing aircraft land at an inner city airstrip (3). Serving the airstrip is a monorail (4) which has a central station (5). From an autotaxi terminal (6) an autotaxi (7) travels, guided by underground cables. Motorists travel on a highway (8) while pedestrians move around the city on a fast three-lane walkway (9). Shorter walkways (10) carry passengers from other transportation to the super train (11), which they board at a special terminal (12). Transportation systems, and their passengers, communicate by radio through a communications dish (13) or by using the network of fiber optic cables (14).

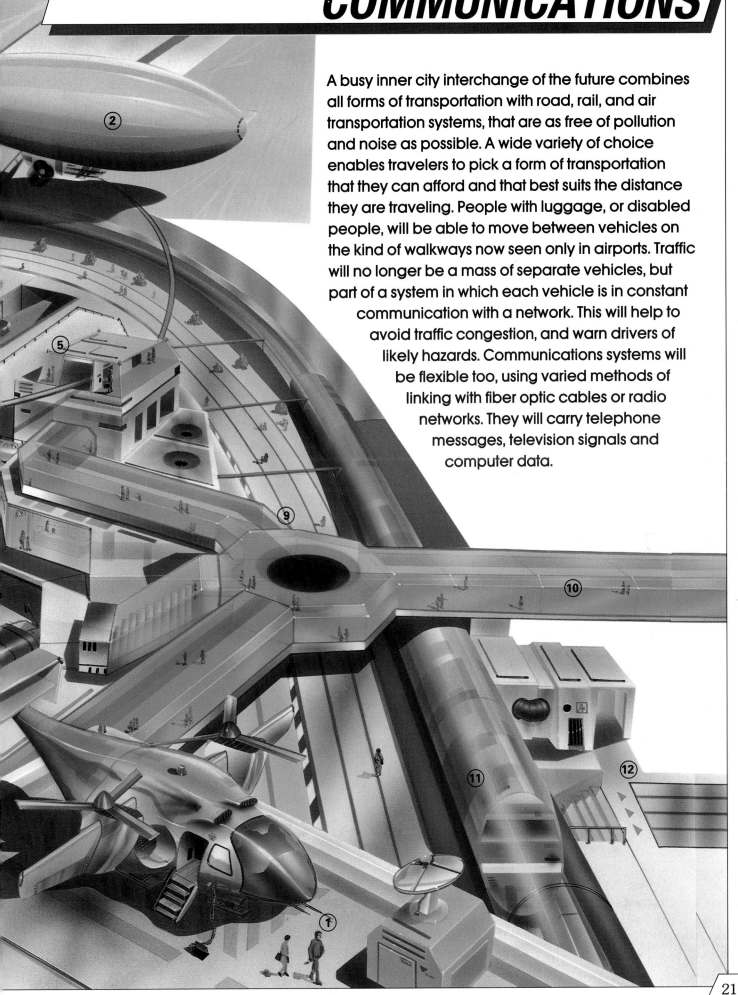

A busy inner city interchange of the future combines all forms of transportation with road, rail, and air transportation systems, that are as free of pollution and noise as possible. A wide variety of choice enables travelers to pick a form of transportation that they can afford and that best suits the distance they are traveling. People with luggage, or disabled people, will be able to move between vehicles on the kind of walkways now seen only in airports. Traffic will no longer be a mass of separate vehicles, but part of a system in which each vehicle is in constant communication with a network. This will help to avoid traffic congestion, and warn drivers of likely hazards. Communications systems will be flexible too, using varied methods of linking with fiber optic cables or radio networks. They will carry telephone messages, television signals and computer data.

Automation

Automatic pilots on aircraft have increased safety and made a pilot's job very much easier, especially on long flights where the pilot's concentration might otherwise falter. Railways have benefited from automation through computer-controlled signaling, allowing higher speeds and more trains along a section of track. Machines can automatically produce a traveler's choice of ticket, and other machines can check the ticket at stations, and collect the ticket if necessary.

Driverless trains, widely used on some London Underground lines, are spreading to other railways. For example, they are used to provide a shuttle service around airports and exhibition centers. A computer controls a network, varying each train's speed as necessary, and stopping it at each station. Sensors tell the computer where each train is, and it makes sure that the trains do not crash into each other.

Machines for issuing automated train tickets

Driverless monorail train (yellow) at an airport

Bullet trains

The original Japanese Bullet Train is a very fast, conventional train. The future bullet train will be much more efficient – it will overcome the problem of a high-speed train's movement being affected by resistance from air in the atmosphere. The bullet train uses air pressure to push it along a sealed tunnel. Pumps in the tunnel create a vacuum in front of the train, and the air pressure behind pushes the train into it. When the train is in a station, special airlocks allow passengers to enter or leave without leaking air into the tunnel. The train itself is pressurized, to stop air leaking from it into the vacuum in front. But building tunnels is very expensive indeed, and this will limit the number of bullet trains.

An experimental Japanese bullet train

Autocars

Autocars are a development of the passenger transporters and robots now used for transportation around factories and other large sites. A control track under the road passes signals to and from the autocar about other vehicles, and the route to be taken. The autocar computer interprets this information, passing instructions to the engine, steering, and brakes. In this way the car is controlled, it is kept at a safe distance from other vehicles, and it turns onto other roads when necessary, perhaps to avoid a traffic jam or to divert around roadworks. A radar sensor at the front of the autocar watches for obstructions or emergencies. In an emergency, the autocar computer will quickly stop the vehicle.

A robot cart for carrying materials in a factory

Computer

Signal device in road

Pickup point

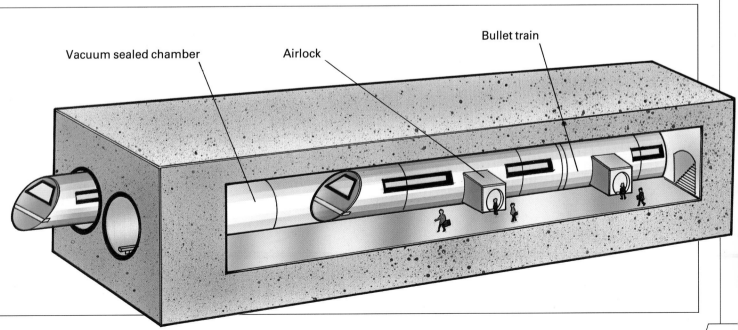

Vacuum sealed chamber

Airlock

Bullet train

Access to the skies

Vertical takeoff and landing (VTOL) aircraft make more city-center airports likely. They avoid or replace long journeys to airports outside cities. VTOL aircraft tilt engines upward for takeoff, and turn them horizontal for normal flight. Short takeoff and landing (STOL) aircraft have big engines and great lift, and can use very short runways. Airships were once dangerous because they used inflammable hydrogen gas for lift. Modern ones use safe helium instead, and new, light engines. They are not very fast, and may be used more for carrying cargo than passengers.

A vertical takeoff and landing aircraft

Optica, a short takeoff and landing craft

A modern helium-filled airship

Space hop

Planes have been proposed that will fly between airports on opposite sides of the Earth, but go into space on the way. The key to their technology is their engines, which will power winged flight in the atmosphere, burning fuel in air. As the aircraft moves out of the atmosphere, the engines start using oxygen, carried on board, instead of air. Soon after reaching space, the aircraft can stop its engines, and coast around the Earth in orbit. When it nears its destination the engines push it toward Earth and guide the aircraft to its landing. The idea combines the advantages of a modern airliner and a space shuttle, using existing airports.

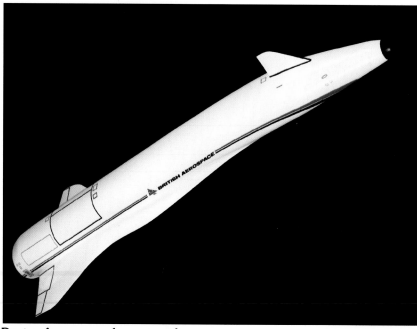

Design for a space-hop aircraft

Communication

For more than 100 years, the telephone has provided voice communication for people who are apart. Recently, fax technology has enabled people to send documents, using telephone lines. Telephone links can now provide full visual communications, as well as sound, and videophones are being used in some places. Each videophone has a small video camera and television screen, corresponding to the microphone and earpiece in a conventional phone. Just as conventional telephones can be used for "conferencing," so videophones can be linked for several people in different areas to communicate with each other. Each videophone sends signals by radio to a communications satellite, which sends the signal on to each of the other videophones in the conference. To see and hear the other conference members, each person will need extra screens and loudspeakers. In a conference involving four videophones, each participant will need a total of three screens and speakers.

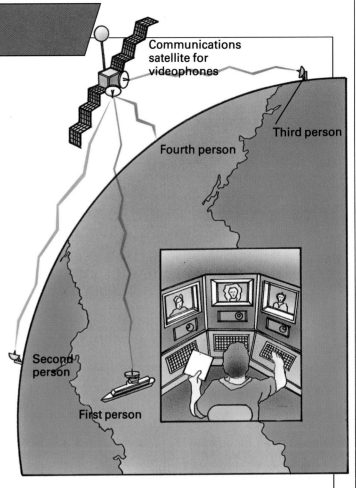

Communications satellite for videophones

Third person

Fourth person

Second person

First person

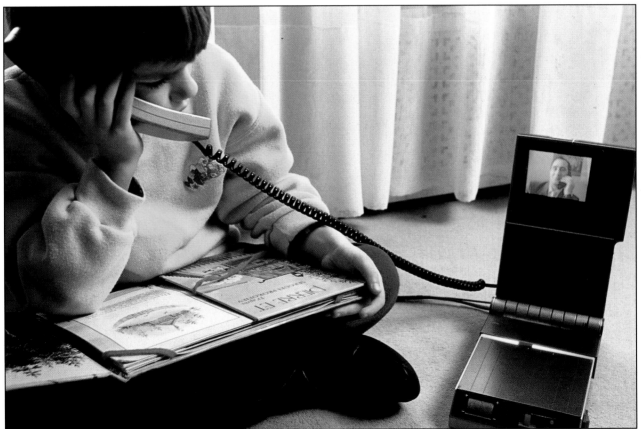

A child using a compact videophone to see and talk to his father

Keeping the Earth clean will be a growing concern for many years to come. This means reducing pollution from factories, power stations, and cars. Building and transportation methods will become more environment-friendly, causing less damage through noise, pollution or waste. Current sources of energy will become scarcer. New, cleaner ways of producing it will develop.

New technology will improve people's living standards in many ways. Machines will continue to bring greater comfort, longer lives, more wealth, and greater choice in entertainment. But the machines will also increase some of the world's problems, and greater emphasis will be needed on solving problems that result from changing technology. For example, machines use energy, particularly as electricity, so more machines will use more energy and make energy scarcer. But years of generating electricity have made the Earth polluted, and electricity generation will have to be done in cleaner ways in future. Other problems to be tackled center on the world's steadily growing population which will produce more mouths to feed, and which will require more use of land for housing and farming.

Future problems

Car pollution will continue to be a problem for many years. Car exhausts are made cleaner by catalytic converters, which will become compulsory in more and more countries. Making cars smaller and lighter makes them burn less fuel, saving energy. But all gasoline-driven cars pollute the atmosphere with carbon dioxide gas. This gas increases the greenhouse effect, making the Earth overheat through retaining more of the Sun's energy. Electric cars do not burn fuel, are quiet, and are environmentally friendly. They look likely to replace many gasoline cars.

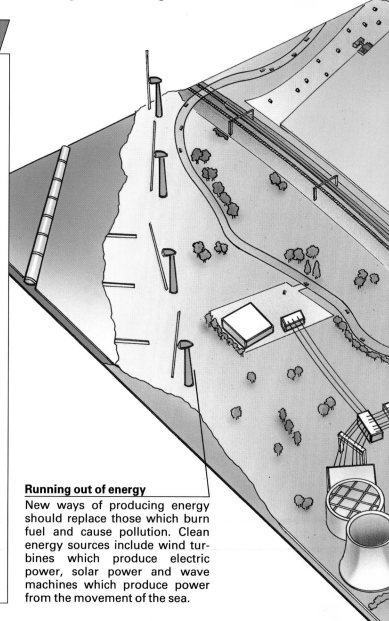

This car produces little carbon dioxide.

Running out of energy

New ways of producing energy should replace those which burn fuel and cause pollution. Clean energy sources include wind turbines which produce electric power, solar power and wave machines which produce power from the movement of the sea.

Feeding the millions?

An increasing population will need more food, and less land will be available on which to grow it. Greater food production can mean more pollution from farms. New, clean ways of producing food, on less land, will be needed.

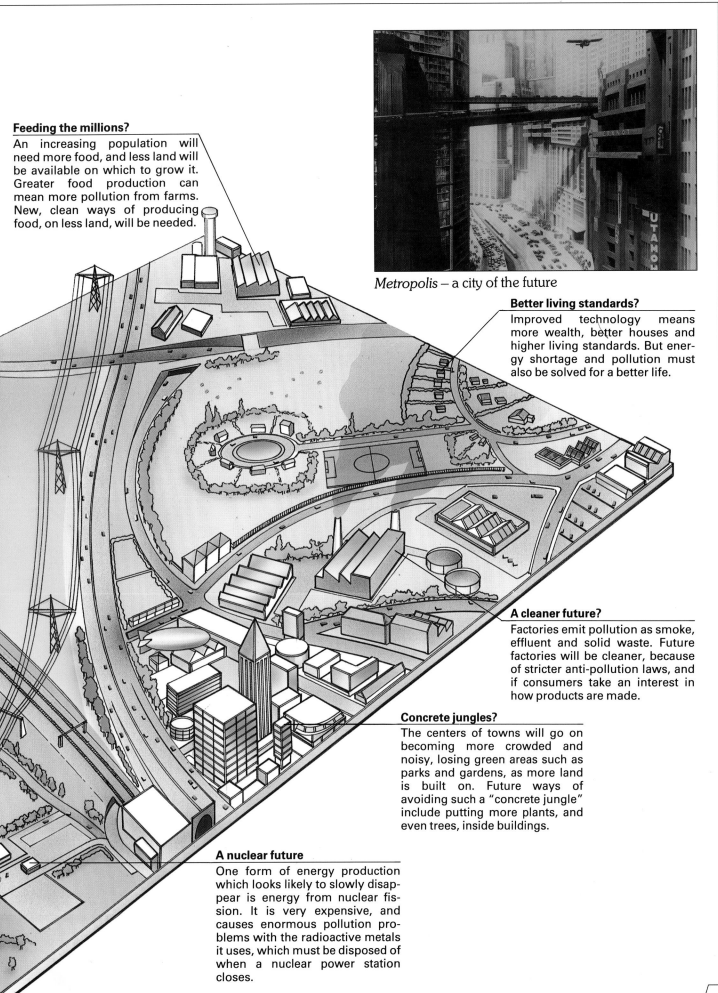

Metropolis – a city of the future

Better living standards?

Improved technology means more wealth, better houses and higher living standards. But energy shortage and pollution must also be solved for a better life.

A cleaner future?

Factories emit pollution as smoke, effluent and solid waste. Future factories will be cleaner, because of stricter anti-pollution laws, and if consumers take an interest in how products are made.

Concrete jungles?

The centers of towns will go on becoming more crowded and noisy, losing green areas such as parks and gardens, as more land is built on. Future ways of avoiding such a "concrete jungle" include putting more plants, and even trees, inside buildings.

A nuclear future

One form of energy production which looks likely to slowly disappear is energy from nuclear fission. It is very expensive, and causes enormous pollution problems with the radioactive metals it uses, which must be disposed of when a nuclear power station closes.

Future energy

Much electricity comes from burning fossil fuels such as coal or oil, supplies of which may eventually run out. The burning produces pollution, causing problems such as acid rain. This can be avoided by making power without burning. Tides and waves in the world's oceans contain energy which can be converted to electricity. Tide turbines across a river mouth or a narrow channel turn tidal energy into electricity. Wave machines make electric power from wave motion. Sea thermal power comes from the Sun's heat on oceans. On land, geothermal power comes from steam created by heat within the Earth. Wind turbines produce electricity, and solar power units turn sunlight into electricity.

Nuclear power comes from nuclear fission, and is the most widely used alternative to fossil fuels. But at present it is expensive, and has pollution problems. A possible future alternative is nuclear fusion, which harnesses the power of the hydrogen bomb.

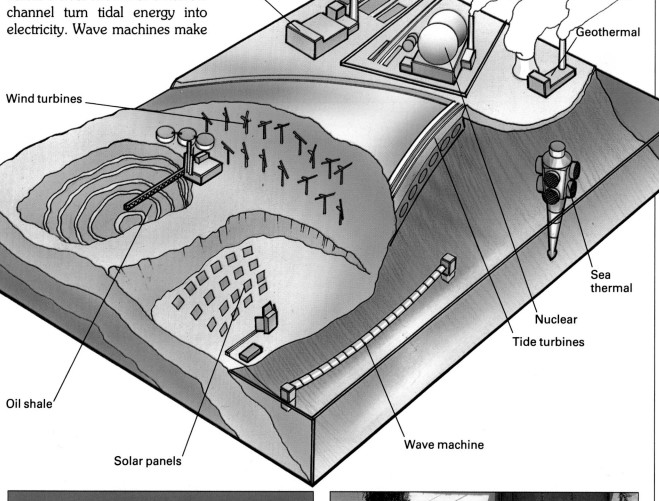

Waste burner

Geothermal

Wind turbines

Sea thermal

Nuclear

Tide turbines

Oil shale

Wave machine

Solar panels

Windmills for generating electricity

Solar panels for heating water

Better use of land

Much of the Earth's land lies empty and unused. Some is waterlogged by being near a river or the sea. Other land is derelict, having been used for mining, industry or disposing of waste. Much more land is unused because it is mountainous, desert or in very cold parts of the world. Unfortunately, land that can be used for the first time, such as tropical rain forest, is running out and there are great problems in using it. Deforestation destroys animal habitats, and increases the amount of carbon dioxide in the atmosphere. The need to make better use of land, because of increasing population, is steadily growing. Answers to these problems include making more land by building dikes to reclaim low-lying areas that at present are under the sea.

A farm with crops growing on reclaimed land in the Netherlands

Cleaner atmosphere

The most dramatic example of the need for the Earth to be cleaner is what is happening in the atmosphere. Industry, power stations and transportation all pour out pollution such as sulphur compounds. The sulphur compounds dissolve in raindrops which fall as acid rain. Much carbon dioxide is converted into oxygen by plants, particularly trees. But the number of trees is falling as forests are cleared for building or farming, or trees are killed by acid rain. So the amount of carbon dioxide in the air is growing. This dirtying of the atmosphere increases the greenhouse effect. Extra carbon dioxide and dust in the air make the atmosphere reflect heat down again. This leads to global warming and to changes in climate.

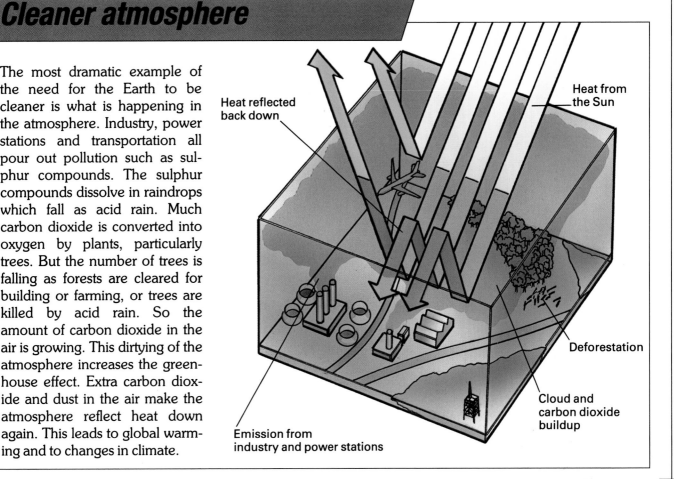

Heat reflected back down

Heat from the Sun

Deforestation

Cloud and carbon dioxide buildup

Emission from industry and power stations

People have already spent more than a year living in space, and construction techniques have been developed for assembling space stations. Provided that the cost of shuttling material into space can be brought down by developing better rockets, these techniques will be used to make orbiting space stations and Moon bases. Some stations will become factories for producing new materials and products that can only be made in zero-gravity conditions, or in a vacuum. Such factories will be automated, running themselves with computer links to Earth. Human beings will be used for activities such as constructing space stations and bases, and carrying out scientific research.

So far, space has been used mainly for research, gaining information about the Moon, Solar System and the Universe. Future possible uses include manufacturing in zero-gravity conditions, mining in space, or even disposing of pollution such as the waste from nuclear reactors. This will need cheap vehicles for transportation into Earth orbit and for traveling the long distances between planets.

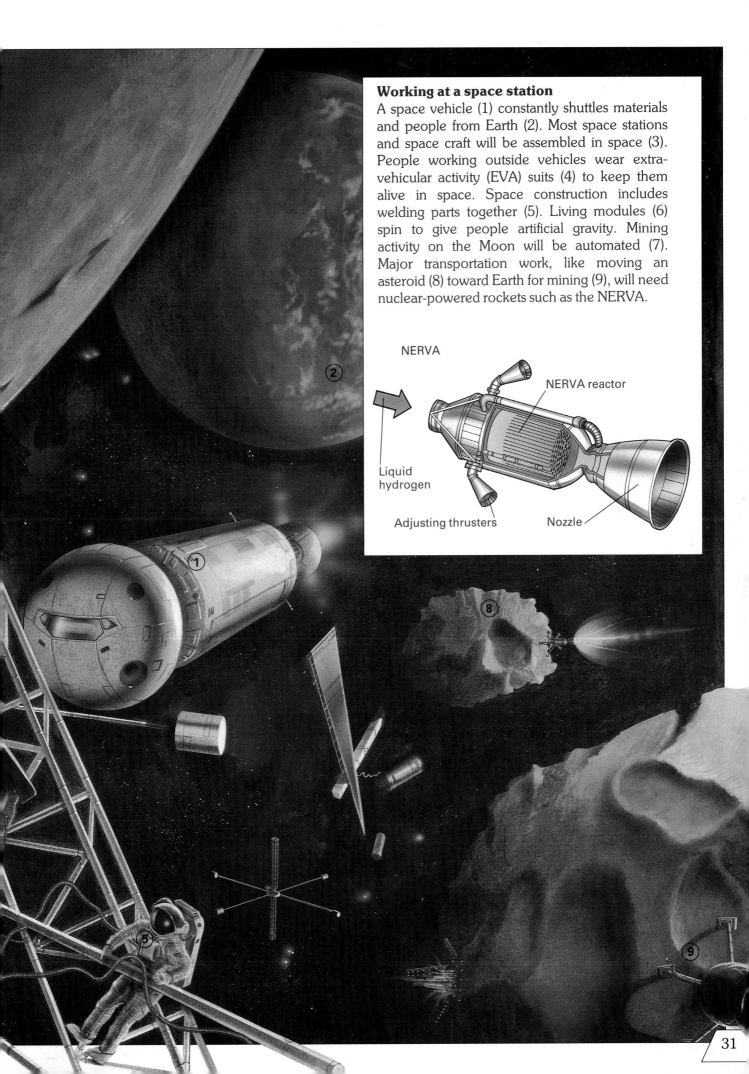

Working at a space station

A space vehicle (1) constantly shuttles materials and people from Earth (2). Most space stations and space craft will be assembled in space (3). People working outside vehicles wear extra-vehicular activity (EVA) suits (4) to keep them alive in space. Space construction includes welding parts together (5). Living modules (6) spin to give people artificial gravity. Mining activity on the Moon will be automated (7). Major transportation work, like moving an asteroid (8) toward Earth for mining (9), will need nuclear-powered rockets such as the NERVA.

NERVA

NERVA reactor

Liquid hydrogen

Adjusting thrusters

Nozzle

Resources

Much of the material for building space stations is available in space. The Moon, for example, has more iron and titanium than the Earth, and has plenty of aluminum and silicon. Much of the material needed to build a large Moon station could be mined and refined there, avoiding the expense of carrying the materials from Earth. On the Moon, solar energy could be used to convert ores into metals for sending back to Earth.

The greatest resource from space is constant sunlight. Huge solar-powered satellites will be able to beam down energy that can be converted into electricity on Earth.

Futuristic Moon-mining colony

A sample of Moon rock

Biosphere

For people to live permanently on the Moon, an artificial biosphere would be built, following the pattern of the Earth's biosphere. The biosphere consists of air, soil, water in rivers and oceans, and the plants and animals they support. Each part of the biosphere is in balance, and the same balances would be needed on the Moon. As the Moon does not have enough gravity to hold an atmosphere, the air of the biosphere would have to be contained within an envelope or cover. The most likely materials to build the envelope are metal and glass, both easily extracted or made from minerals obtained on the Moon. The envelope, like the Earth's upper atmosphere, would have to shield the lower parts from the Sun's ultraviolet light. Water, nitrogen and carbon, all essential for life, would be transported from Earth, and constantly recycled within the biosphere. Water evaporating in the lower biosphere, for example, would form clouds or condense on the envelope at night, running down it to form streams at its base. Plants would be grown within the biosphere to produce oxygen and food. To avoid pollution, energy could be produced outside the biosphere from solar panels, and all machines, including transportation, would be electric-powered.

Volunteers leave an artificial biosphere built on Earth

Space colonies

Colonies in space, orbiting around the Earth or another planet, would need to be huge to be able to support permanent inhabitants. There would be plenty of energy from solar panels, but all materials for building and for sustaining life would have to be transported to the colony from Earth or the Moon. Once the space colony was operational, all its contents would be carefully conserved and recycled. Plants would be grown in sunlight to make oxygen from carbon dioxide breathed out by human beings. Water could be recycled and distilled to purify it using solar energy. For the comfort of inhabitants, and for their convenience in working and moving around, artificial gravity would be created by making the space colony spin about its axis. Once started, it would keep spinning. Stations with a larger radius or a faster spin would have greater gravity.

Artist's impression of a future space colony

Work on the Space Shuttle

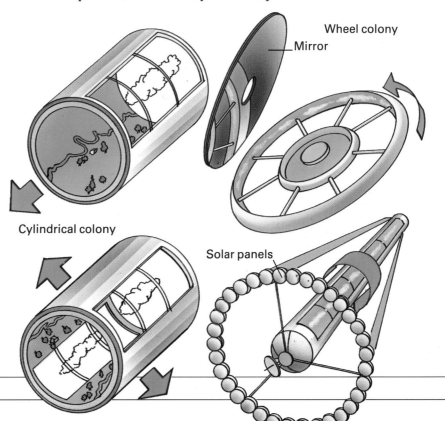

Cylindrical colony

Wheel colony

Mirror

Solar panels

33

Looking into the future to guess what will happen is not easy. Most of the items in this book simply assume the technology – ways of doing things – that is already developed will be used more widely in the future. No doubt the new products that appear in the next 25 years will affect people's lives as much as the changes brought by video machines, robots in industry, or air travel have in the previous generation's lives. But predicting changes is a matter of guesswork.

Computers – a safe bet

It is easy to assume that computers will be used more and more widely, and will be built in to more and more appliances, and even into buildings such as homes. For 20 years or so, computers have been steadily improving, becoming cheaper, and have been ever more widely used. Cheap new input devices such as a joystick or a mouse have been added. It seems reasonable to expect that input direct from the human voice will follow shortly, making a keyboard unnecessary. Size will go on reducing. With wallet-sized computers available at the beginning of the 1990s, it seems likely that watch-sized computers will be common by the end of the 1990s.

Guessing about computer application is more difficult. Ten years ago, the Prestel system was just starting up in Britain, using telephone lines to link offices and homes with information computers. Anyone looking at the system then would have seen quite a cheap system allowing families to communicate with each other on their television screens, or order goods at any time of the day or night. They might have guessed that by now millions of homes would have installed one. In some countries, such as France and Japan, that has happened, but in Britain the proportion of homes on such a system is small.

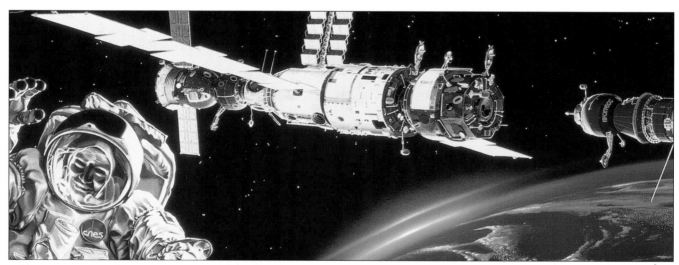

Fact: the Soviet MIR space station in orbit

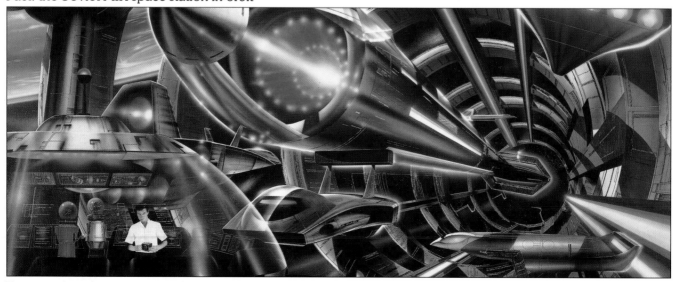

Fantasy: Artist's impression of a rotating space colony

GLOSSARY

alternative energy method of producing electrical or heat energy for homes or workplaces as an alternative to burning fossil fuels or using nuclear energy.

autocar driverless car controlled by a computer and a control track built into the road.

automation production of goods by machines that control themselves and operate without any human assistance.

biomass organic matter, mainly from plants, used as a source of energy by burning or decaying to produce an inflammable gas.

biosphere parts of the Earth (or any other planet or heavenly body) that support life – requiring air, water, and soil.

bullet train train that runs in a tunnel, and is propelled mainly by air pressure in a way similar to that in which a bullet is forced along a gun barrel.

CAT scan abbreviation of Computerized Axial Tomography. This is a method of using X rays to take "pictures" of a section through the human body.

computer machine that solves problems by processing information according to a set of instructions called a program. Many computers solve problems relating to control of other devices and machines.

environment all of the conditions in which a plant or animal lives. It includes the atmosphere and soil, as well as the effects of other plants and animals. It often refers to the environment of all life on Earth.

fax abbreviation of facsimile transmission, a method of sending copies of a document along a telephone line to a distant receiver.

fiber optics method of sending signals or images by passing light along glass-fiber cables.

fossil fuel material formed inside the Earth from decayed plant or animal matter, and which can be burnt to produce heat. The main fossil fuels are coal, natural gas, and petroleum.

greenhouse effect warming of the atmosphere caused by heat that has been radiated or reflected from the Earth's surface being reflected down by a layer of carbon dioxide in the atmosphere.

hologram a three-dimensional image of an object produced using lasers.

hydroponics technique for growing plants by suspending the plant with its roots hanging in a solution of nutrients.

laser device for producing a strong, narrow beam of single-color light which can be directed very precisely.

laser surgery medical technique that involves use of lasers for operations such as welding a detached retina or destroying a tumor.

light-sensitive describing materials that have surfaces which change in some way, such as generating an electric current, when light strikes them.

microsurgery surgery in which special instruments are used under a microscope or similar device.

pollution change in the biosphere caused by the release of poisonous or harmful substances, so making the environment unsafe or destroying it.

recycling reusing materials, such as paper or glass, by collecting them after they have been used, and processing them to help to make new paper or glass.

resource anything which is in limited supply, such as fuels for energy or iron, and which can be used to make or move something.

robot machine that can sense, pick up, and move objects, and that can perform other operations on them. Robots can control themselves, following a pattern set by a computer.

service industry business that provides a service rather than goods. Examples are tourism and retailing.

short takeoff and landing (STOL) aircraft airplane that needs only a short runway for takeoff and landing.

simulator computer-controlled machine that creates sensory impressions, for example, of flying an aircraft.

technology application of science to produce a solution to a practical or industrial problem.

vertical takeoff and landing (VTOL) aircraft airplane that can take off with no runway.

videophone type of telephone that transmits moving video pictures of users, in addition to speech.

voice synthesizer device that uses a computer to artificially produce the sounds of human speech.

INDEX

All entries in bold are found in the Glossary

Photographic Credits:
Cover and pages 6, 8 bottom, 9 left, 16 top and 33: J. Allan Cash; intro pages and pages 7, 8 top, 9 right, 10 all, 11 all, 12, 14, 16 bottom, 19 bottom, 22 middle and bottom, 23, 24 middle right, 25, 28 right, 32 top left, 33 and 34 top: Science Photo Library; pages 9 bottom, 18 right and 32 bottom left: Robert Harding Library; pages 13 top, 17, 18 bottom, 29 and 32 right: Topham Picture Library; pages 13 bottom and 27: British Film Institute; page 19 top: Solo Syndication; page 22 top: Eye Ubiquitous; page 24 left and middle left: Aviation Picture Library; page 24 bottom: British Aerospace; page 26: Times Newspaper; page 28 left: Zefa; page 34 bottom: Alex Pang.